Buttons, Hooks & Eyes

Holly Crawford

Lokke Press
New York

ISBN 978-0-9852461-0-5

For my late father, William C. Shissler, Jr.

& George Crawford

Post-it—

I have taken my ticket.

Common patrimony—

They meet at a party.

She bore him a son.

Adam knew Eve was his wife.

Five baby strollers—

Now Adam knew Eve was his wife

married yesterday, my wife's keeping her name.

 I have a private practice of psychiatry in Scarsdale;

my three step-children live near the Sea of Galilee.

I'm there five days every month.

My own children live in Westchester.

 Abel is the keeper of sheep

Remarried about five years ago,

 and Cain, a tiller of the ground.

Previous marriage... ended in divorce.

Three dogs—

Give me something to do with my hands,

a painting, a poem, an Angus cow-calf operation

with forty cows, three dogs, and an old house.

One and the same civilization produces two such different things.

All are on the order

and ostensibly, parts of the same,

here, however, their connections seems to end.

Does the fact that a disparity such exists

Exists within the frame of a single culture

indicate this is the natural order?

Or is it something entirely new,

and particular to our age?

Band-aid—

I reached the epitome of success in talent shows
combining singing with board breaking.
Unfortunately, I injured my shoulder.
I'm now a broken down mediocre tennis player.
Shall I be a fugitive and wanderer on the earth.

Maybe my daughter will support me.

A-1 sauce—

Up in time for lunch…
spent most of the day resting…
then, off for a steak dinner.

Art and loose change—

I am still working on the Sidewinder missile program.
Complex devices and an art that I find interesting,
A relationship between aesthetic experience,
 the individual, and the social.

One red umbrella—

A society, as it becomes less and less able,
in the course of its development,
to justify its particular forms,
important issues are left untouched.

A political kidnapper had me in front of an AK-47
and very much wanted to pull the trigger.
Did you ever think of the zillions of leaves
  that come into our view in the fall?
Every fall, every year?

Two tricycles—

I went to the opera for a nickel.
While I was there, over two hundred people,
mostly civilians, were killed.

How strange that this could happen
 to a chronically healthy child.
We'd thought most diseases had been covered
by shots or outgrown.

Narrowing and raising to the expression of an absolute
all relatives and contradictions
 resolved or beside the point.
We must not be deceived by superficial phenomena.

Old houses and chocolate—

Hence it developed

the most important function was to find a path.

To keep culture moving, in the midst

of ideological confusion and violence.

I moved to California, came out and

bought and sold old houses.

After that, I was alone with my chocolate.

I guess you had to be there.

The shopping carts—

It is time we look into the whys and wherefores.

I spent seven years doing research.

Every now and then, I give a speech where people seem interested,

But at dinner parties I've learned not to talk too much.

Hot water bottles—

Marriage endures,
children develop independence,
parents age and pass on.

Still waiting ….
I cope with insufficient exercise and excess paper.

Seventeen cars—

Attempting to keep communications functioning,
and dust out of the whiskey.
 Broken by too many recollections.

Post-it II—

Arrested and thrown in jail for four hours.

Ideas about money and taxes.

Film and Transparencies—

I remember struggling with Nino Scalia over a note
And scuffling with him over some soap.

Red and White Billiard Ball Stripped—

I authorized the import of 500,000 handguns.
Rationalization came easily
There were already 200,000,000 handguns in the country.

Days spent visiting lovely austere churches
 and abandoned manor houses....
Out the window a tractor plows a field
I hunger for my friends.

Train schedules—

Lunch on the terrace
lots of time to sit and think.
A talk about government with the doorman
 things in general
the cute little shields along the streets
against the buildings
and the beautiful train stations.

Transitional Objects—

Changed collecting interests
Down come quilts, up go rugs.

Post-It III—

I have figured out what a book titled
Dewey, Women and Feminism should look like.

Take-out menu—

Same cork screw, same job,

same wife, same house

   we still like classical music and French wine,

      but not yet a vegetarian.

   I love a medium-rare steak.

Button, Hooks & Eyes—

We met for lunch.
Plates flew, tables tipped.
We never really broke up.

Lounge Chairs and Back Stairs—

Up at noon
Brandy Egg Nog for breakfast.
A visit to a French movie in first class,
Silly Symphony was the only thing I could understand
Back to the man with the bushy eye-brows ....

Postcard—

Five years ago on Monday at 5:05 p.m.
I woke up.

Back of an Envelope—

I am writing on too many subjects
poetics of intimacy,
whatever the occasional verse-maker diehard will pounce.

One deflated ball—

Years rolled on years
 and after turning fifty, with plastic surgery
I had hoped to leave behind on the carousel
 that is guarded by the clown
a good deal of baggage.

Empty Bottle—

I apologize tremendously for having to tell you this
 in an email, but

Mother died yesterday.

I love you...

I´m sorry that I had to tell you through an email,
 but your phone number is on my powerbook.

Post-it IV—

I've been compiling data on marathon-related deaths,
black mittens with yellow strips.

Hooks and Eyes—

I actually do wish that I could be there
 with you… to help you through your grief and sorrow,
 to help sort out all of their personal belongings.
 I do not wish to see them just thrown away either.
I've been there
 all of the boxes
the memories that you will have to deal with,
 the vivid memories.
 FileMaker issues.
 Lots of sleepless nights.

Remote control—

These accidental and isolated instances
have fooled people. And then
those puzzling borderline cases appear.
The net result is always to the detriment of true culture, in any case.
Please accept my sincere apology
 for going against Mother's wish,
of not telling Holly when she passed away.
 And I do hope someday,
 possibly when you get over the emotions
you're experiencing now that it is the right thing to do.
The same point can be made with respect to kitsch literature: it
provides vicarious experience.
 And Eddie Guest and the *Indian Love Lyrics,*
which are more poetic.

Stacked chairs—

I received this email and an enclosure from Barbara.
Note: I copied and appended the letter rather than having to deal
with .zip files.

Your mother was a dear, dear lady.
She was always friendly and outgoing.
I am happy to have been able to spend time around her.
She actually declared herself my "second mom."

Tim, having been his mother's caretaker, is
particularly overwhelmed.
  As for the daughter,
Holly deserves to be told that her mother passed away.

Please know that you are welcome to attend the memorial service
next Sunday,
May 15, from 11-2.

 It is my privilege to be hostess for this event.
 More and more people are saying they want to attend.
 People liked and loved your mother.

I've attached a letter to your sister.

PLEASE, please, please forward it to her.

Cards and Letters—

You don't know me, but
 please accept my sympathies at the death of your mother.

We had even spent recent holidays together.
Tim is overwhelmed.
I am holding an informal Memorial Service
 Brunch is from 11 to 2 pm.

You are invited to attend.

Please appreciate that I'm trying to empathize with you.
Along with your husband and any other family or friends,
though I don't quite know how since I don't know you.

 I've been told there is a rift
and that you are currently out of the country.
 All of that aside, I know you would want to be invited.
Your mother was a very nice lady
 If there's anything I can do, relative to family dynamics
 or anything else.

Please let me know.

The Cell phone —

The echoing silence is punctuated
by the neatness of this antithesis,
 which is more contrived;
it corresponds to and defines the tremendous interval
that separates.
The interval is too great to be closed
by all the infinite.

Postcard III—

Sharpening the chainsaw,
 we are growing weary of distractions.
We're feed up seeking solace from a satellite.

Postcard IV—

I conducted two performances of an opera

Nobody got hurt.

I couldn't tell you when it's likely to happen again.

Post-It V—

Whether or not the avant-garde could possibly flourish
 not pertinent at this point.

Files—

Two months later, I emerged from a coma with total amnesia and
became immediately unemployed.

A jade vase dislodged by automatic weapon fire landed on my head
my memory has now returned,
but each morning   I wake up acoustically obsessed with the
question: how in the future,
lacking a stern but stabilizing influence,
will Abū Dhabbah do?

We can see then that although from one point of view
the personal is not accidental to the roles they play,
from another point of view it is only an incidental factor.

Acknowledgements

Red and White Billiard Ball Stripped and *Two tricycles* are re-printed here from *Van Gogh's Ear*. I would like to thank them. Reading of these works at CBGB in NYC, just before it close, was arranged by Ian Aryes and Philip Ward.

This project was started in January 2002 and was not finished until recently.

Holly Crawford is an artist, writer and curator (**www.art-poetry.info**). She is the Director and founder of AC Institute an experimental spaces for research and exhibition in contemporary art (**www.artcurrents.org**) and publication of books on contemporary art and criticism. She taught art and art issue in the UCLA Art Department and at SVA. She received her Ph.D. from the University of Essex in Art History and Theory, B.A and M.A. in Economics and M.S. in Behavioral Science from UCLA. From 2004-2006, she was a non-clinical Fellow at NYU Medical School Psychoanalytic Center. She was born in California and now lives in New York. Member AICA, CAA, & Art Table.

Publications:

Outsourced Critics, Holly Crawford, project by & editor, essays by Jill Connor and Stephen Squibb, AC Institute, 2010; "Who Gets to Play?' in *Popular Culture Values and the Arts Essays on Elitism versus Democratization*, edited by Ray B. Browne and Lawrence A. Kreiser, McFarland, 2009; Catalogue essay "Disney and Pop Art",for the catalogue *Once Upon a Time Disney*, Grand Palais and Fine Art Museum, Montreal, 2008; *Artistic Bedfellows* (editor), UPA/Roman & Littlefield, 2008; "Temporary Bedfellows: Claes Oldenburg, Maurice Tuchman and Disney," essay in *Artistic Bedfellows*, 2008; "Having Their Cake and Eating It Too: The case of Christo's and Jeanne-Claude's Im(permanence) and Exclusivity," essay in *Artistic Bedfellows*, 2008 (conference paper Carnegie Mellon); "Disney and Pop Art", *Once Upon a Time Disney*, Bruno Girveau, (Editor & Curator) Grand Palais and Fine Art Museum, Montreal (two editions-one in French and one in English) Prestel, 2007; *Attached to the Mouse, Disney and Contemporary Art* (2006) UPA/Roman & Littlefield, 2006; "What's New," catalogue essay, DIVA (Digital and Video Art Fair), Paris, 2005, and assorted chapbooks starting in 1995.